Keeping Fit

Teaching Tips

Turquoise Level 7

This book focuses on the grapheme /c/.

Before Reading

- Discuss the title. Ask readers what they think the book will be about. Have them support their answer.
- Ask readers to sort the words on page 3. Read the words together. Reinforce that /c/ can have a hard /k/ sound or a soft /s/ sound.

Read the Book

- Encourage readers to read independently, either aloud or silently to themselves.
- Prompt readers to break down unfamiliar words into units of sound and string the sounds together to form the words. Then, ask them to look for context clues to see if they can figure out what these words mean. Discuss new vocabulary to confirm meaning.
- Urge readers to point out when the focused phonics grapheme appears in the text. Does it have a hard /k/ sound or a soft /s/ sound?

After Reading

- Ask readers comprehension questions about the book. In what ways were people in the book exercising to keep fit?
- Encourage readers to think of other words with the /c/ grapheme. On a separate sheet of paper, have them write the words in two columns: one for the hard /k/ sound and the other for the soft /s/ sound.

© 2024 Booklife Publishing
This edition is published by arrangement with Booklife Publishing.

North American adaptations © 2024 Jump!
5357 Penn Avenue South
Minneapolis, MN 55419
www.jumplibrary.com

Decodables by Jump! are published by Jump! Library.
All rights reserved. No part of this book may be reproduced in any form without written permission from the publisher.

Library of Congress Cataloging-in-Publication Data is available at www.loc.gov or upon request from the publisher.

ISBN: 979-8-88524-769-6 (hardcover)
ISBN: 979-8-88524-770-2 (paperback)
ISBN: 979-8-88524-771-9 (ebook)

Photo Credits

Images are courtesy of Shutterstock.com. With thanks to Getty Images, Thinkstock Photo and iStockphoto. Cover – Shutterstock. p4–5 – Niyazz, Angelo Giampiccolo. p6–7 – Ana Flasker, cktravels.com. p8–9 – Wirestock Creators, Dirk M. de Boer, COULANGES. p10–11 – BlueOrange Studio, Wasim Khuzam. p12–13 – gorillaimages, FooTToo. p14–15 – Odua Images, Monkey Business Images. p16 – Shutterstock.

Can you sort these words into two groups? One group has c as in **cat**. One group has c as in **face**.

Decide

Doctor

Cone

Fact

Count

Pencil

Place

Cent

It is important to stay fit. We can stay fit with sports and exercise. Do you have a sport that you like to do?

This girl is running.

First, we must make sure that we eat and drink specific things. Milk has a lot of calcium in it. Calcium helps our bones stay strong.

Running is a good way to stay fit. We can run with other people. We can run in a race. Racing is exciting!

Step up to the line, get set . . . go!

Are you quick at running? If you have the pace to win a race, you could run against people in a marathon. A marathon is a long race.

What was the most recent sport you saw? Did you see soccer? In soccer, you need skill to score. Soccer keeps us fit.

There is a lot of running in soccer. We run to an open space for a player to pass the ball. We face the goalie and shoot to win.

There are a lot of sports to do. Ice hockey is different from a lot of sports. We play ice hockey on an ice rink, with ice skates on our feet.

It is normal to slip. It can hurt, so you must brace yourself if you fall on the ice! If you fall twice, do not let it stop you!

Can you bend a lot? If you can, you could be an acrobat. Acrobats must keep fit to perform. You can see acrobats at the circus.

The circus is cool. Acrobats can flip and spin in a hoop. You need to do specific training to be in the circus.

This acrobat is upside down!

Do not say no the next time you get asked to exercise. It is good for you. Go see what sports you can do to keep fit.

You might win a race with people in class. You might turn into a circus acrobat. You might win a soccer match. These are good ways to keep fit!

Say the name of each object below. Is the "c" in each an /s/ sound or a /k/ sound?

cow

circle

celery

coat